Taste of Christmas

Have Yourself a
Toasty Little Christmas

Compiled by Snapdragon Group℠, Tulsa, Oklahoma.

ISBN 978-1-62416-134-6

Published by Barbour Publishing, Inc., P.O. Box 719, Uhrichsville, Ohio 44683, www.barbourbooks.com

Our mission is to publish and distribute inspirational products offering exceptional value and biblical encouragement to the masses.

Member of the
Evangelical Christian
Publishers Association

Printed in the United States of America.

Taste of Christmas

Have Yourself a Toasty Little Christmas

Recipes and Holiday Inspiration for Bread Lovers

BARBOUR
PUBLISHING

The smell of good bread baking,
like the sound of lightly flowing water,
is indescribable in its evocation
of innocence and delight.

M. F. K. FISHER

Contents

Therefore the Lord himself
shall give you a sign;
Behold, a virgin shall conceive,
and bear a son,
and shall call his name Immanuel.

ISAIAH 7:14

The word *bread* appears 361 times in the King James Version of the Bible. The words "give us this day our daily bread" are also included in the model prayer Jesus gave His disciples. In fact, bread in all its forms has been deemed so essential to human health and well-being that it is called the "staff of life." What better season than Christmas to showcase bread in all its glory?

This little book includes tasty bread recipes for Christmas giving, sharing, and serving—along with breads that play a role in Christmas celebrations around the world. We hope these recipes will enhance your Christmas delight and add a few new favorites to your holiday table.

Have yourself a toasty little Christmas as you celebrate the newborn King!

It is more blessed
to give than to receive.

Christmas Breads for Giving

It's not how much we give but
how much love we put into giving.

MOTHER TERESA

Maple-Pumpkin Loaf

Prep Time: 20 minutes
Cook Time: 1 hour
Oven Temperature: 350 degrees

Preparation Tip: Stop mixing while batter is still lumpy.
Yield: 18 servings

INGREDIENTS:

1 stick butter, softened to room temperature
1 cup maple syrup
2 eggs
1¼ cups pumpkin puree
1 teaspoon pure vanilla

1½ cups flour
1 teaspoon baking powder
1 tablespoon pumpkin pie spice
1 teaspoon cinnamon
¼ teaspoon salt
½ cup chopped pecans

Instructions:

In large bowl, cream butter, maple syrup, eggs, pumpkin, and vanilla. In separate bowl, combine flour, baking powder, pumpkin pie spice, cinnamon, and salt. Stir well. Add pecans. Carefully fold in butter mixture, just until blended. Spoon into 8.5 x 4.5-inch, parchment-lined loaf pan. Bake for 1 hour. Cool on wire rack for 10 minutes. Remove from pan and cool completely. Wrap and store overnight before slicing.

Cherry-Walnut Pumpkin Bread

Prep Time: 20 minutes
Cook Time: 1 hour
Oven Temperature: 350 degrees

Preparation Tip: Grease bottom and
only ½ inch up sides of loaf pan.
Yield: 16 to 18 servings

INGREDIENTS:

2 eggs

⅓ cup cherry juice

3 tablespoons canola oil

⅔ cup water

1 (14 ounce) package pumpkin
  quick-bread mix

½ cup walnuts, chopped

½ cup dried cherries

¾ cup powdered sugar

3–4 teaspoons cherry juice

¼ cup dried cherries

Instructions:

Whisk eggs in large bowl. Add cherry juice, oil, and water. Whisk until smooth. Add pumpkin quick-bread mix and stir with wooden spoon until completely incorporated. Add walnuts and ½ cup dried cherries. Spoon into greased 8 x 4 x 2-inch loaf pan. Spread evenly and bake for 1 hour or until wooden toothpick inserted near the center comes out clean. Cool on wire rack for 10 minutes. Remove from pan. Cool completely. Stir together powdered sugar and cherry juice until drizzle consistency. Pour over loaf. Sprinkle with remaining dried cherries. Wrap and store overnight before slicing.

Chocolate Pecan Bread

Prep Time: 25 minutes
Cook Time: 50 minutes
Oven Temperature: 350 degrees

Preparation Tip: Wrap in red cellophane and add a sprig of greenery.
Yield: 12 to 14 servings

INGREDIENTS:

2 cups flour
½ cup sugar
1 tablespoon baking powder
½ teaspoon salt
1 egg
¾ cup milk

½ cup canola oil
1 cup semisweet chocolate chips
1 cup pecans, chopped
⅓ cup milk chocolate chips
½ teaspoon shortening
⅓ cup pecans, chopped

INSTRUCTIONS:

In large bowl, combine flour, sugar, baking powder, and salt. Blend well. Make well in center of flour mixture and set aside. In another bowl, beat egg with fork. Stir in milk and oil. Add egg mixture to flour mixture. Stir until moistened. Fold in 1 cup of chocolate pieces and 1 cup of pecans. Batter will be lumpy. Spoon batter into an 8 x 4 x 2-inch loaf pan. Bake for 1 hour. Cool on wire rack for 10 minutes. Remove from pan and cool completely. Wrap and store overnight. Before serving, combine remaining chocolate chips and shortening in a saucepan over low heat. Stir until melted and smooth. Drizzle chocolate mixture over loaf. Sprinkle additional chopped nuts on top. Let stand until chocolate is set.

Holiday Fruit Loaf

Prep Time: 30 minutes
Cook Time: 65 minutes
Oven Temperature: 350 degrees

Preparation Tip: Storing overnight at room temperature makes flavors mellow and loaf easier to slice.
Yield: 12 to 14 servings

INGREDIENTS:

2 cups flour

1 cup sugar

2 teaspoons baking powder

½ teaspoon salt

1 teaspoon orange peel, finely shredded

2 eggs

½ cup milk

1 stick butter, melted

¾ cup cranberries, chopped

¾ cup walnuts, toasted and chopped

½ cup dried figs or dates, chopped

Instructions:

In large bowl, stir together flour, sugar, baking powder, and salt. Stir in orange peel. Make well in center of flour mixture. Set aside. In another bowl, whisk together eggs, milk, and melted butter. Add egg mixture to flour mixture. Stir until moistened. Batter will be lumpy. Stir in cranberries, walnuts, and figs or dates. Spoon batter into greased 8 x 4 x 2-inch loaf pan. Spread evenly. Bake for 65 minutes or until wooden toothpick inserted near the center comes out clean. You may need to cover with foil the last 15 minutes. Cool on wire rack for 10 minutes. Remove from pan. Cool completely. Wrap and store overnight before slicing.

Grandma's Apple Pie Bread

Prep Time: 35 minutes
Cook Time: 1 hour
Oven Temperature: 350 degrees

Preparation Tip: You will need about 4 medium apples.
Yield: 12 to 14 servings

INGREDIENTS FOR BREAD:

1 stick butter, softened
1 cup sugar
¼ cup buttermilk
2 teaspoons baking powder
2 eggs
1 teaspoon vanilla

2 cups flour
½ teaspoon salt
2 cups apples, shredded, peeled
1 cup walnuts, chopped
½ cup golden raisins

INGREDIENTS FOR STREUSEL TOPPING:

¼ cup brown sugar, packed
3 tablespoons flour

2 tablespoons butter
⅓ cup walnuts, chopped

INSTRUCTIONS:

In large bowl, cream butter and sugar together. Add buttermilk and baking powder. Beat with electric mixer until combined. Add flour and salt. Beat until combined. Stir in apple, nuts, and raisins. Spoon batter into greased 9 x 5 x 3-inch loaf pan. Spread evenly. Combine sugar and flour for streusel topping. Cut butter into topping with pastry blender. Stir in walnuts. Sprinkle streusel over bread batter. Bake for 1 hour or until toothpick inserted near center comes out clean. Cool on wire rack for 10 minutes. Remove from pan and cool completely. Wrap and store overnight before slicing.

Eggnog Bread

Prep Time: 25 minutes
Cook Time: 50 minutes
Oven Temperature: 350 degrees

Preparation Tip: No matter what size pan you use, fill it no more than ⅔ full.
Yield: 12 to 14 servings

INGREDIENTS FOR BREAD:

2¼ cups flour

2 teaspoons baking powder

½ teaspoon salt

¼ teaspoon ground nutmeg

2 eggs

1 cup sugar

1 cup eggnog

½ cup (1 stick) butter, melted

1 teaspoon vanilla

½ teaspoon rum extract

1 cup slivered almonds, toasted

INGREDIENTS FOR EGGNOG ICING:

½ cup powdered sugar

¼ teaspoon vanilla

Dash ground nutmeg

2 to 3 teaspoons eggnog

Instructions:

In large bowl, combine flour, baking powder, salt, and nutmeg. In another bowl, whisk eggs. Stir in sugar, eggnog, melted butter, vanilla, and rum extract. Add egg mixture to flour mixture. Stir just until moistened. Batter will be lumpy. Fold in toasted almonds. Spoon batter into one 9 x 5 x 3-inch loaf pan or two 7½ x 3½ x 2-inch loaf pans. For large loaf pan, bake for 50 to 55 minutes. For smaller pans, bake for 40 to 45 minutes or until toothpick inserted near center comes out clean. Cool on wire rack for 10 minutes. Remove from pan(s). Cool completely. Wrap and store overnight. An hour before serving, combine powdered sugar, vanilla, and nutmeg. Stir in enough eggnog to create a thin icing. Drizzle over bread. Let icing set.

Christmas Cinnamon Bread

Prep Time: 30 minutes
Cook Time: 45 minutes
Oven Temperature: 350 degrees

Preparation Tip: Run a wide rubber spatula down through batter and up in a circular motion to marble.
Yield: 12 to 14 servings

INGREDIENTS:

½ cup pecans, finely chopped

2 teaspoons ground cinnamon

1⅓ cups sugar

2 cups flour

1 teaspoon baking powder

½ teaspoon salt

1 egg

1 cup milk

⅓ cup cooking oil

Instructions:

In small bowl, combine nuts, cinnamon, and ⅓ cup of sugar. Set aside. In large bowl, combine remaining sugar, flour, baking powder, and salt. Make well in center of flour mixture. Set aside. In another bowl, whisk egg. Whisk in milk and oil. Add egg mixture to flour mixture. Stir until moistened. Batter will be lumpy. Pour half the batter into 9 x 5 x 3-inch loaf pan. Sprinkle with half the cinnamon mixture. Repeat with remaining batter and cinnamon mixture. Use rubber spatula to create marbling. Bake 45 to 50 minutes or until toothpick inserted near the center comes out clean. Cool on wire rack for 10 minutes. Remove from pan and cool completely. Wrap and store bread overnight before slicing.

Date Nut Bread

Prep Time: 25 minutes
Cook Time: 50 minutes
Oven Temperature: 350 degrees

Preparation Tip: Buy whole, unsugared dates.
Yield: 12 to 14 servings

INGREDIENTS:

2 cups flour
1 cup sugar
1 tablespoon baking powder
½ teaspoon salt
1 egg

1¼ cups milk
¼ cup canola oil
1 cup mixed nuts, chopped
½ cup dates, pitted and chopped

INSTRUCTIONS:

In large bowl, stir together flour, sugar, baking powder, and salt. Make well in center of flour mixture. Set aside. In another bowl, whisk egg. Whisk milk and oil into egg. Add egg mixture to flour mixture until moistened. Batter will be lumpy. Fold in nuts and dates. Spoon batter into greased 8 x 4 x 2-inch, parchment-lined loaf pan. Spread evenly. Bake for 50 to 55 minutes or until toothpick inserted near center comes back clean. Cool on wire rack for 10 minutes. Remove from pan and cool completely. Wrap and store overnight before slicing.

Raisin and Rum Christmas Bread

Prep Time: 90 minutes
Cook Time: 50 minutes
Oven Temperature: 375 degrees

Preparation Tip: Loaf is done if it sounds hollow when tapped on the underside.
Yield: 12 to 14 servings

INGREDIENTS:

⅔ cup raisins
3 tablespoons water
1 teaspoon rum extract
3 tablespoons sugar
1 cup warm milk
2 packages dry yeast
4 cups flour

1 teaspoon salt
6 tablespoons butter
2 eggs
Grated peel of 1 lemon
1 cup almonds, toasted and chopped
1 egg yolk, beaten

Instructions:

Mix raisins, water, and rum extract in a bowl. Cover and set aside. In another bowl, stir 1 teaspoon sugar into milk and sprinkle with yeast. Let stand 5 minutes or until surface is frothy. Stir to moisten any remaining dry particles. In small bowl, melt butter. Cool slightly. In medium bowl, combine remaining sugar, butter, eggs, and lemon peel. Stir in yeast mixture. Incorporate flour until a soft dough forms. Add almonds. On floured surface, knead dough until smooth (5 to 10 minutes). Cover and let rise in warm place until double in size (30 minutes). Place dough in 12 x 4-inch loaf pan. Let rise 30 minutes. Brush with egg yolk. Bake 40 to 50 minutes. Cool on wire rack for 10 minutes. Remove from pan and cool completely.

Festive Blueberry Bread

Prep Time: 30 minutes
Cook Time: 50 minutes
Oven Temperature: 350 degrees

Preparation Tip: This recipe will make 4 small loaves.
Yield: 12 to 14 servings

INGREDIENTS:

1½ cups flour
1½ teaspoons cinnamon
½ teaspoon salt
½ teaspoon baking soda
¼ teaspoon baking powder
¼ teaspoon nutmeg

1 egg
¾ cup brown sugar, packed
½ cup orange juice
⅓ cup canola oil
1 cup pecans, chopped
½ cup dried blueberries

Instructions:

In large bowl, combine flour, cinnamon, salt, baking soda, baking powder, and nutmeg. Make well in center of flour mixture. Set aside. In another bowl, whisk egg. Stir in sugar, orange juice, and oil. Add egg mixture to flour mixture, stirring until moistened. Batter will be lumpy. Fold in nuts and berries. Spoon batter into four 4½ x 2½ x 1½-inch pans. Spread evenly. Bake for 25 to 28 minutes or until toothpick inserted in center comes out clean. Cool on wire rack for 10 minutes. Remove from pan. Cool completely. Wrap and store overnight before slicing.

Cherry-Almond Holiday Bread

Prep Time: 30 minutes
Cook Time: 1 hour
Oven Temperature: 350 degrees

Preparation Tip: Tossing fruit in flour
will keep it from sinking.
Yield: 12 to 14 servings

INGREDIENTS:

6 ounces dried cherries

1 tablespoon flour

3 cups flour

1 tablespoon baking powder

1¼ teaspoon allspice

1 teaspoon salt

3 eggs

1¾ cups sugar

¾ cup canola oil

⅓ cup milk

2 teaspoons vanilla

1½ cups chopped almonds

Instructions:

Toss cherries in 1 tablespoon of flour. Set aside. Combine flour, baking powder, allspice, and salt in large bowl. Make well in center of flour mixture. Set aside. In another bowl, whisk eggs. Add sugar, oil, milk, and vanilla and whisk together. Add egg mixture to flour mixture and stir until moistened. Fold in cherries and almonds. Batter will be lumpy. Spoon batter into two 8 x 4 x 2-inch, parchment paper-lined loaf pan. Bake for 60 to 65 minutes or until toothpick inserted near center comes out clean. Cool on wire rack for 10 minutes. Remove from pan and cool completely. Wrap and store overnight before slicing.

Walnut Banana Bread

Prep Time: 20 minutes
Cook Time: 1 hour, 15 minutes
Oven Temperature: 350 degrees

Preparation Tip: This recipe can be made with white or whole wheat flour.
Yield: 12 to 14 servings

INGREDIENTS:

1 stick plus 2 tablespoons butter, softened
½ cup plus 3 tablespoons sugar
3 eggs
3 bananas
¼ teaspoon vanilla

1½ cups flour
2 teaspoons baking powder
¼ teaspoon salt
1 cup walnuts, chopped
3 tablespoons milk

Instructions:

In medium bowl, cream butter and sugar until fluffy. Beat in eggs, one at a time. Peel and mash bananas with fork. Stir bananas and vanilla into creamed mixture. Sift together flour, baking powder, and salt. Add walnuts to flour mixture. Fold flour mixture into creamed mixture. Add milk. Pour batter into greased 9 x 5 x 3-inch loaf pan. Spread evenly. Bake for 1 hour and 15 minutes or until toothpick inserted near center comes out clean. Cool on wire rack for 10 minutes. Remove from pan. Cool completely. Wrap and store overnight before slicing.

Orange Nut Bread

Prep Time: 30 minutes
Cook Time: 1 hour
Oven Temperature: 350 degrees

Preparation Tip: Mixed nuts work well in this recipe.
Yield: 12 to 14 servings

INGREDIENTS:

1¼ cups flour, sifted

2 teaspoons baking powder

½ teaspoon baking soda

¾ teaspoon salt

1 cup sugar

¾ cup nuts

½ cup raisins

¼ cup orange rind, grated and chopped

1 egg, well beaten

½ cup milk

½ cup orange juice

2 tablespoons shortening, melted

Instructions:

Sift together flour, baking powder, baking soda, salt, and sugar. Add nuts, raisins, and orange rind. Combine egg, milk, and orange juice. Add to flour mixture. Add shortening. Mix until all flour is dampened and fruit and nuts are well distributed. Spoon batter into greased 9 x 5 x 3-inch loaf pan. Bake for 1 hour or a toothpick inserted near center comes out clean. Cool on wire rack for 10 minutes. Remove from pan. Cool completely. Wrap and store overnight before slicing.

Mrs. Santa's Sweet Caraway Bread

Prep Time: 30 minutes
Cook Time: 1 hour
Oven Temperature: 350 degrees

Preparation Tip: Caraway seeds are a
favorite in holiday baking. However,
they are not seeds but the small,
ripe fruit of the caraway plant.
Yield: 12 to 14 servings

INGREDIENTS:

1¾ cups flour, sifted
2 teaspoons baking powder
¼ teaspoon salt
½ stick butter
¾ cup sugar

1 egg, unbeaten
¾ cup milk
1 tablespoon caraway seeds
¾ teaspoon vanilla

Instructions:

Sift together flour, baking soda, and salt. In large bowl, cream butter, adding sugar gradually until mixture is fluffy. Add egg and beat well. Alternately add a small amount of flour mixture and then a small amount of milk, beating after each until smooth. Add caraway seeds and vanilla. Blend well. Spoon batter into 9 x 5 x 3-inch loaf pan lined with greased parchment paper. Bake for 1 hour or until toothpick inserted near center comes out clean. Cool on wire rack for 10 minutes. Remove from pan. Cool completely. Wrap and store overnight before slicing.

Holiday Cinnamon Apple Bread

Prep Time: 30 minutes
Cook Time: 1 hour
Oven Temperature: 350 degrees

Preparation Tip: Make sure to remove all apple and orange seeds.
Yield: 12 to 14 servings

INGREDIENTS:

½ orange, peeled and chopped
2 cups apples, peeled and chopped
1 cup nuts, coarsely chopped
1 tablespoon flour
4 cups flour
2 teaspoons baking soda
1 teaspoon cinnamon

1 teaspoon nutmeg
2 cups sugar
1 cup oil
4 teaspoons buttermilk
1 teaspoon vanilla
1 teaspoon lemon juice

INSTRUCTIONS:

Toss orange bits, apples, and nuts in 1 tablespoon of flour. Set aside. Sift together flour, baking soda, cinnamon, and nutmeg. Set aside. Whisk together sugar, oil, buttermilk, vanilla, and lemon juice. Pour into flour mixture and stir well. Add orange bits, apples, and nuts and stir well. Spoon into greased 9 x 5 x 3-inch loaf pan. Bake for 1 hour or until toothpick inserted near center comes out clean. Cool on wire rack for 10 minutes. Remove from pan. Cool completely. Wrap and store overnight before slicing.

Do not neglect to do good
and to share what you have.

HEBREWS 13:16 NRSV

Christmas Muffins for Sharing

Those who bring sunshine into the lives of others cannot keep it from themselves.

JAMES M. BARRIE

Apple Spice Muffins

Prep Time: 20 minutes
Cook Time: 25 minutes
Oven Temperature: 425 degrees

Preparation Tip: Make sure to remove apple seeds.
Yield: 14 muffins

INGREDIENTS:

3 cups flour
4 teaspoons baking powder
3 tablespoons sugar
2 teaspoons salt
½ cup shortening
2 eggs

1¼ cups milk
1 cup chopped apples
1 tablespoon flour
2 tablespoons sugar
¼ teaspoon cinnamon

Instructions:

Sift together flour, baking powder, sugar, and salt. Cut in shortening. Whisk together eggs and milk. Toss apples in 1 tablespoon of flour. Add to egg mixture. Add egg mixture to flour mixture and stir only until moistened. Spoon into paper cup-lined muffin tin. Combine sugar and cinnamon and sprinkle over the top of muffins. Bake for 25 minutes. Cool completely on wire rack.

Orange Raisin Muffins

Prep Time: 20 minutes
Cook Time: 25 minutes
Oven Temperature: 425 degrees

Preparation Tip: Plumping raisins makes them soft and moist.
Yield: 14 muffins

INGREDIENTS:

⅔ cup raisins
2 teaspoons orange juice
1 teaspoon honey
3 cups flour
4 teaspoons baking powder
3 tablespoons sugar

2 teaspoons salt
½ cup shortening
2 eggs
1¼ cups milk
1½ teaspoon orange rind
2 tablespoons sugar

Instructions:

Place raisins in microwave-safe container. Pour orange juice and honey over them and place plastic wrap over the top of container. Microwave on *high* for 30 to 45 seconds. Let stand for 1 to 2 minutes before removing plastic wrap. Set aside. Sift together flour, baking powder, sugar, and salt. Cut in shortening. Whisk together eggs and milk. Add raisins and orange rind to egg mixture. Add egg mixture to flour mixture and stir only until moistened. Spoon into paper cup–lined muffin tin. Sprinkle sugar over the top of muffins. Bake for 25 minutes. Cool completely on wire rack.

Blueberry Oat Bran Muffins

Prep Time: 20 minutes
Cook Time: 25 minutes
Oven Temperature: 375 degrees

Preparation Tip: When using frozen berries, thaw on paper towels to absorb juice.
Yield: 10 to 12 muffins

INGREDIENTS:

1½ cups flour

¾ cup oat bran

1 tablespoon baking powder

½ teaspoon salt

⅓ cup canola oil

1 egg

⅔ cup light brown sugar, packed

½ cup milk

¾ cup fresh or frozen blueberries, thawed

2 tablespoons course sugar

INSTRUCTIONS:

Sift together flour, oat bran, baking powder, and salt in large bowl. In separate bowl, combine oil, egg, brown sugar, and milk. Stir well. Make well in center of flour mixture and add milk mixture. Stir just until dry ingredients are incorporated. Fold in blueberries carefully with as few strokes as possible. Line 12-cup muffin tin and spoon batter into cups (no more than ⅔ full). Bake for 10 minutes at 400 degrees and another 15 at 375 degrees. Cool on wire rack for 10 minutes before removing the muffins from the pan.

Razzle-Dazzle Raspberry Muffins

Prep Time: 20 minutes
Cook Time: 30 minutes
Oven Temperature: 375 degrees

Preparation Tip: Place a small pan with
½ cup water in oven while baking.
The moisture will add some crustiness
to the muffins.
Yield: 12 to 14 muffins

INGREDIENTS:

3½ cups flour
4 teaspoons baking powder
½ teaspoon baking soda
1 teaspoon salt
1⅓ cups sugar
2 eggs

1 stick butter, melted
1 cup milk
1 cup buttermilk
1½ teaspoons vanilla
1½ cups fresh or frozen raspberries,
    thawed

INSTRUCTIONS:

Sift together flour, baking powder, baking soda, and salt in large bowl. Set aside. In separate bowl, stir together sugar, eggs, and butter, reserving 2 tablespoons of sugar for later. Whisk milk, buttermilk, and vanilla into egg mixture. Make well in center of flour mixture and add egg mixture to it. Stir just until dry ingredients are incorporated. Fold in raspberries carefully with as few strokes as possible. Line 12-cup muffin tin with muffin cups and spoon batter to top of paper liners. You may have some extra batter. Sprinkle with remaining sugar. Bake for 30 minutes. Cool on wire rack for 10 minutes before removing muffins from pan.

Christmas Morning Muffins

Prep Time: 20 minutes
Cook Time: 22 minutes
Oven Temperature: 375 degrees

Preparation Tip: Eat these muffins the first day or freeze them for later.
Yield: 12 muffins

INGREDIENTS:

2 cups flour

⅔ cup sugar

2½ teaspoons baking powder

½ teaspoon salt

¼ teaspoon nutmeg

1 egg

1 cup milk

½ stick plus 1 tablespoon butter, melted

1 teaspoon vanilla

1 cup sugar

1 teaspoon cinnamon

Instructions:

Sift together flour, sugar, baking powder, salt, and nutmeg in large bowl. In separate bowl, whisk together egg, milk, butter, and vanilla. Make well in center of flour mixture and add egg mixture to it. Stir just until batter is evenly blended. Line 12-cup muffin tin with muffin cups and fill each ⅔ full. Bake for 22 minutes or until golden brown. Cool on wire rack for 10 minutes before removing muffins from pan. Mix together butter, sugar and cinnamon. Dip top of each muffin in butter mixture.

Chocolate Pecan Muffins

Prep Time: 20 minutes
Cook Time: 35 minutes
Oven Temperature: 350 degrees

Preparation Tip: Eat these muffins the first day or freeze them for later.
Yield: 12 muffins

INGREDIENTS:

4 (1 ounce) squares semisweet chocolate

1 (1 ounce) square unsweetened chocolate

1½ sticks butter

1 cup sugar

¼ cup dark brown sugar, firmly packed

4 eggs

1 teaspoon vanilla

¼ teaspoon almond extract

¾ cup flour, sifted

1 cup pecans, chopped

Instructions:

Melt chocolate with butter over low heat. Pour chocolate mixture into large bowl and add sugars. Stir well. Beat in 1 egg at a time. Add extracts. Stir well. Add flour a small portion at a time, just until all the dry ingredients are incorporated. Fold in pecans. Spoon batter into lined muffin pan, filling cups almost to the top. Bake for 35 minutes. Cool on wire rack for 10 minutes before removing from pan.

Dutch Cranberry Muffins

Prep Time: 20 minutes
Cook Time: 25 minutes
Oven Temperature: 350 degrees

Preparation Tip: Use your hand to pack down the topping on each muffin before baking.
Yield: 12 muffins

INGREDIENTS:

1½ cups flour

2 teaspoons baking powder

1 teaspoon cinnamon

⅛ teaspoon salt

1 stick butter, melted

¼ cup sugar

¼ cup brown sugar, firmly packed

1 egg

½ cup milk

1 teaspoon vanilla

1¼ cups cranberries

¼ cup pecans, finely chopped

¼ cup dark brown sugar, firmly packed

3 tablespoons flour

1 teaspoon cinnamon

3 tablespoons butter, melted

Instructions:

Sift together flour, baking powder, cinnamon, and salt. Make well in center and set aside. Cream butter with sugars. Stir in egg, milk, and vanilla. Add to flour mixture and stir just until dry ingredients are incorporated. Fold in cranberries. Spoon batter into lined muffin pan, filling cups almost to the top. Combine pecans, brown sugar, flour, and cinnamon. Add butter and stir until mixture takes on a crumbly texture. Spoon mixture over each muffin. Bake for 25 minutes. Cool on wire rack for 10 minutes before removing from pan.

Carrot Cake Muffins

Prep Time: 30 minutes
Cook Time: 35 minutes
Oven Temperature: 350 degrees

Preparation Tip: Even when using paper liner cups, spray the top of the muffin tin with non-stick spray.
Yield: 12 muffins

INGREDIENTS:

1¼ cups flour

1 teaspoon baking powder

½ teaspoon baking soda

1 teaspoon cinnamon

¼ teaspoon nutmeg

½ teaspoon salt

1½ sticks butter

½ cup dark brown sugar, firmly packed

1 egg, beaten

1 tablespoon water

2 cups grated carrots

2 tablespoons coarse sugar

Instructions:

In large bowl, sift together flour, baking powder, baking soda, cinnamon, nutmeg, and salt. Make well in center and set aside. Cream butter with sugar until fluffy. Add egg and water. Beat well. Stir in carrots. Add to flour mixture and stir just until dry ingredients are incorporated. Spoon batter into lined cups of muffin pan, filling each almost to the top. Bake for 35 minutes. Sprinkle tops with sugar and cool on wire rack for 10 minutes before removing from pan.

Merry Cherry Muffins

Prep Time: 50 minutes
Cook Time: 20 minutes
Oven Temperature: 350 degrees

Preparation Tip: Use dry cherries rather than fresh.
Yield: 16 muffins

INGREDIENTS:

1 cup dried cherries
1 cup plain yogurt
1 teaspoon vanilla
1¾ cups flour
2 teaspoons baking powder
1 teaspoon baking soda
⅛ teaspoon salt
1 stick butter, softened
¾ cup sugar
2 eggs

Instructions:

Combine cherries with yogurt and vanilla. Let stand for 20 minutes. In large bowl, sift together flour, baking powder, baking soda, and salt. Make well in center and set aside. In separate bowl, cream butter with sugar until fluffy. Add eggs, 1 at a time, beating after each. Fold in cherry mixture. Then add creamed mixture in several portions and stir just until dry ingredients are incorporated. Fill lined cups of muffin tin ⅔ full. Bake for 10 minutes. Cool on wire rack for 10 minutes before removing from muffin pan.

Pumpkin Pie Muffins

Prep Time: 20 minutes
Cook Time: 15 minutes
Oven Temperature: 400 degrees

Preparation Tip: Cooked or canned pumpkin will work equally well.
Yield: 14 muffins

INGREDIENTS:

1¾ cups flour

1 teaspoon baking soda

1½ teaspoon cinnamon

1 teaspoon nutmeg

¼ teaspoon salt

1 stick butter, softened

¾ cup dark brown sugar, firmly packed

⅓ cup molasses

1 egg

1 cup pumpkin

¼ cup golden raisins

Instructions:

Sift together flour, baking soda, cinnamon, nutmeg, and salt. Make well in center and set aside. In separate bowl, cream butter with sugar until fluffy. Add molasses and stir well. Add egg and pumpkin and stir until well blended. Add creamed mixture to flour mixture in several portions, stirring just until dry ingredients are incorporated. Fold in raisins. Spoon batter into lined muffin pan, filling paper cups ¾ full. Bake for 15 minutes. Cool on wire rack for 10 minutes before removing from pan.

Banana Nut Muffins

Prep Time: 20 minutes
Cook Time: 25 minutes
Oven Temperature: 375 degrees

Preparation Tip: The riper the bananas, the better the muffins.
Yield: 10 to 12 muffins

INGREDIENTS:

2 cups flour
1 teaspoon baking powder
1 teaspoon baking soda
¼ teaspoon salt
½ teaspoon cinnamon
¼ teaspoon nutmeg

3 overripe bananas
1 egg
⅓ cup dark brown sugar, firmly
    packed
¼ cup canola oil
¼ cup pecans or walnuts, chopped

Instructions:

Sift together flour, baking powder, baking soda, salt, cinnamon, and nutmeg. Set aside. In large bowl, beat bananas on *medium* speed or mash with potato masher. Beat in egg, sugar, and oil. Add dry ingredients to banana mixture in portions on *low* speed just until dry ingredients are incorporated. Stir in nuts. Spoon into lined muffin pan, filling each cup ⅔ full. Bake for 25 minutes. Place on wire rack to cool for 10 minutes before removing from pan.

Maple Leaf Muffins

Prep Time: 30 minutes
Cook Time: 22 to 25 minutes
Oven Temperature: 350 degrees

Preparation Tip: For best results, eggs should be room temperature.
Yield: 20 muffins

INGREDIENTS:

1¼ cups pecans, coarsely chopped

2½ cups flour

1 teaspoon baking powder

1 teaspoon baking soda

¼ teaspoon salt

¼ teaspoon cinnamon

½ cup sugar

⅓ cup light brown sugar, firmly packed

3 tablespoons maple syrup

1 stick plus 3 tablespoons butter, softened

3 eggs

1¼ cups buttermilk

60 pecan halves

Instructions:

Toast pecans in oven at 350 degrees for 5 minutes. Allow to cool. Chop and set aside. Sift together flour, baking powder, baking soda, salt, and cinnamon. Set aside

In large bowl, combine sugars, syrup, and butter. Beat with electric mixer on medium until fluffy. Add eggs, 1 at a time, beating after each. Add a portion of buttermilk and then a portion of dry ingredients to butter mixture. Continue to alternate until all has been incorporated. Fold in pecans. Spoon batter into lined muffin pan, filling cups ⅔ full. Press three pecan halves into the top of each muffin. Bake for 22 to 25 minutes or until golden. Cool on wire rack for 10 minutes before removing from pan.

Mocha Chocolate Chip Muffins

Prep Time: 20 minutes
Cook Time: 18 minutes
Oven Temperature: 400 degrees

Preparation Tip: For richer flavor use espresso powder.
Yield: 18 muffins

INGREDIENTS:

- 2 cups flour
- ⅔ cup sugar
- 3 tablespoons unsweetened cocoa powder
- 1½ teaspoons baking powder
- ¼ teaspoon baking soda
- ½ teaspoon cinnamon
- ¼ teaspoon salt
- 1½ teaspoons instant coffee crystals
- 1⅓ cups buttermilk
- 1 egg
- ½ cup canola oil
- ¾ cup semisweet chocolate chips
- ¼ cup pecans, chopped

Instructions:

In large bowl, sift together flour, sugar, cocoa, baking powder, baking soda, cinnamon, salt, and coffee crystals. Make well in center of dry mixture. Set aside. In separate bowl, combine buttermilk, egg, and oil. Add to dry mixture. Stir just until dry ingredients are moistened. Fold in chocolate chips and nuts. Spoon batter into lined muffin tin, filling each cup to ¾ full. Bake for 18 minutes. Cool on a wire rack for 10 minutes before removing from muffin pan.

Peaches and Cinnamon Muffins

Prep Time: 20 minutes
Cook Time: 25 minutes
Oven Temperature: 425 degrees

Preparation Tip: Use fresh peaches only.
Yield: 14 muffins

INGREDIENTS:

3 cups flour

4 teaspoons baking powder

3 tablespoons sugar

2 tablespoons cinnamon

2 teaspoons salt

½ cup shortening

2 eggs, beaten

1 cup fresh peaches, chopped

1¼ cups buttermilk

2 tablespoons sugar

2 teaspoons cinnamon

Instructions:

In large bowl, sift flour, baking powder, sugar, cinnamon, and salt. Make well in center and set aside. In separate bowl, cut in shortening with pastry blender. Add eggs 1 at a time, stirring well after each. Add peaches and stir well. Add a portion of buttermilk and then a portion of dry ingredients to shortening mixture. Continue to alternate just until all dry ingredients have been incorporated. Spoon batter into lined muffin pan, filling cups ⅔ full. Bake for 25 minutes. Cool on a wire rack for 10 minutes before removing from pan.

Each one of you should use whatever gift
you have received to serve others, as faithful
stewards of God's grace in its various forms.

1 PETER 4:10 NIV

Christmas Rolls for Serving

If you're serving people delicious food,
they won't complain.

SALLY SCHNEIDER

Christmas Dinner Rolls

Prep Time: 2 hours, 20 minutes
Cook Time: 15 to 20 minutes
Oven Temperature: 400 degrees

Preparation Tip: Hollow places in rolls result when air bubbles aren't carefully worked out of the dough.
Yield: 2 to 3 dozen, depending on size.

INGREDIENTS:

1 package dry yeast
¼ cup warm water
¾ cup hot milk
3 tablespoons shortening
3 tablespoons sugar

1¼ teaspoons salt
1 egg, beaten
4 cups all-purpose flour
2 tablespoons butter, melted

Instructions:

Sprinkle yeast in warm water, stirring occasionally until foamy. Set aside.
Mix milk, shortening, sugar, and salt in large bowl. Cool to lukewarm.
Stir in yeast and beaten egg. Add 2 cups flour and beat until smooth.
Gradually stir in remaining flour until all is incorporated. On floured
surface, knead dough until it's smooth and elastic (8 to 10 minutes).
Place in large buttered bowl. Turn over once to grease upper side of
dough. Cover dough and let rise in warm place until double (about 1
hour). Press dough down into bowl to remove air bubbles. Butter hands
and divide dough into small pieces. Roll into balls and place on greased
baking pan with sides. They should be touching. Cover with cloth and
let rise until double (about 45 to 60 minutes). Bake at 400 degrees for
15 to 20 minutes. Remove from oven and brush with melted butter
while hot.

Festive Buttermilk Rolls

Prep Time: 1 hour, 40 minutes
Cook Time: 15 to 20 minutes
Oven Temperature: 400 degrees

Preparation Tip: Additional flour can be added to make dough easier to handle.
Yield: 18 rolls

INGREDIENTS:

1 cup buttermilk, room temperature

1½ teaspoons sugar

¼ teaspoon baking soda

3 tablespoons shortening

2 packages dry yeast

2½ cups flour, sifted

1 teaspoon baking powder

1 teaspoon salt

Instructions:

Combine milk, sugar, baking soda, and shortening. Stir until shortening is softened. Add yeast and stir to dissolve. Sift together flour, baking powder, and salt. Add to milk mixture in two portions. With your hands, work flour into dough until it is manageable. Turn out onto floured surface, cover, and let stand for 10 minutes. Knead for 8 minutes or until dough is smooth. Pull off pieces of dough and roll into balls. Place on greased cookie sheet, close enough to touch. Cover with damp cloth and let rise in warm spot until double (about 1 hour). Bake at 400 degrees for 18 minutes.

Refrigerator Rolls

Prep Time: 1 day (for refrigeration),
2 hours, 30 minutes
Cook Time: 15 minutes
Oven Temperature: 400 degrees

Preparation Tip: Use a 2½-inch biscuit
cutter.
Yield: 18 rolls

INGREDIENTS:

1¾ cups warm water

2 packages dry yeast

½ cup sugar

1 tablespoon salt

1 egg

½ stick butter, softened

6 cups flour, sifted

1 tablespoon butter, melted

Instructions:

Sprinkle yeast over warm water and stir until all dry particles are moistened. Add sugar and salt. Stir until dissolved. Add egg, softened butter, and 3 cups of flour. Beat at *medium* speed for 2 minutes, or until smooth. Gradually add 1 cup flour, beating hard after each addition. Using your hands, work remaining flour into dough until smooth. Brush top of dough with melted butter. Cover with moistened towel. Let rise in refrigerator until double in bulk (2 hours). Punch down dough and refrigerate for 1 to 3 days. Punch dough down once a day. On floured surface, roll out ⅓ of dough to a ⅜-inch thickness. Cut with biscuit cutter. Brush with melted butter. Place 1 inch apart on greased cookie sheet. Cover with towel and allow to rise until double in bulk (1 hour). Brush rolls again with melted butter. Bake for 12 to 15 minutes.

Cheesy Dinner Rolls

Prep Time: 2 hours, 20 minutes
Cook Time: 15 to 20 minutes
Oven Temperature: 400 degrees

Preparation Tip: Any hard, grated cheese will do well.
Yield: 2 to 3 dozen, depending on size

INGREDIENTS:

1 package dry yeast

¼ cup warm water

¾ cup hot milk

3 tablespoons shortening

3 tablespoons sugar

1¼ teaspoons salt

1 egg, beaten

4 cups flour

1 cup cheddar cheese, grated

2 tablespoons butter, melted

Instructions:

Sprinkle yeast in warm water, stirring occasionally until foamy. Set aside. Mix milk, shortening, sugar, and salt in a large bowl. Cool to lukewarm. Stir in yeast and beaten egg. Add 2 cups flour and beat until smooth. Gradually stir in remaining flour and cheese until all is incorporated. On floured surface, knead dough until it's smooth and elastic (8 to 10 minutes). Place in large buttered bowl. Turn over once to grease upper side of dough. Cover dough and let rise in warm place until double (about 1 hour). Press dough down into bowl to remove air bubbles. Butter hands and divide dough into small pieces. Roll into balls and place on greased baking pan with sides. They should be touching. Cover with cloth, and let rise until double (about 45 to 60 minutes). Bake at 400 degrees for 15 to 20 minutes. Remove from oven and brush with melted butter while hot.

Jolly Squash Rolls

Prep Time: 2 hours, 45 minutes
Cook Time: 12 to 15 minutes
Oven Temperature: 450 degrees

Preparation Tip: Acorn, butternut, hubbard, spaghetti, or any winter squash will work.
Yield: 18 rolls

Ingredients:

1 cup milk

2 tablespoons sugar

1¼ teaspoons salt

2 tablespoons shortening

1 package dry yeast

¾ cup mashed, cooked winter squash

3½ to 4 cups flour, sifted

2 tablespoons butter, melted

Instructions:

In saucepan over low heat, stir together milk, sugar, salt, and shortening until shortening melts. Cool to lukewarm. Stir in yeast and squash. Stir in enough flour to make soft dough. Place in greased bowl and turn once to oil all sides. Cover with towel. Let rise in warm place until double in bulk (1 hour). Punch down dough. Cover bowl with damp dish towel and let rise in warm place until double in bulk, about 30 minutes. Pull off pieces of dough and roll into balls. Place on greased cookie sheet, close enough to touch. Cover with damp cloth and let rise in a warm spot until double (about 1 hour). Bake at 450 degrees for 12 to 15 minutes. Remove from oven and brush with melted butter while hot.

Holiday Potato Rolls

Prep Time: 2 hours, 45 minutes
Cook Time: 12 to 15 minutes
Oven Temperature: 450 degrees

Preparation Tip: These are best when refrigerated overnight before baking.
Yield: 4 dozen rolls

INGREDIENTS:

6 tablespoons sugar

6 tablespoons butter

2½ teaspoons salt

½ cup hot mashed potatoes

1¼ cups milk, scalded

1 package dry yeast

¼ cup warm water

¼ teaspoon baking soda

1 teaspoon baking powder

5 cups flour

2 tablespoons butter, melted

1 tablespoon sea salt

INSTRUCTIONS:

Combine sugar, butter, salt, and potatoes in large bowl. Add milk and beat at *medium* speed with electric mixer. Set aside until lukewarm. Combine yeast and warm water. Stir until all dry particles are moistened. Set aside until foamy. Combine yeast mixture, baking soda, and baking powder with milk mixture and beat well. Add enough flour to form stiff dough. Cover and let dough rise for 15 minutes. Add remaining flour until dough is stiff and no longer sticky. Knead until dough is smooth. Place in buttered bowl, turning once to oil dough on all sides. Cover and refrigerate for 1 day or overnight. Punch down dough. Shape into balls and place 1 inch apart on greased cookie sheet. Cover and allow dough to rise for 1 hour. Brush tops with butter and sprinkle with sea salt. Bake for 15 to 20 minutes or until golden brown.

Sweet Tater Rolls

Prep Time: 2 hours, 30 minutes
Cook Time: 20 minutes
Oven Temperature: 400 degrees

Preparation Tip: Removing the peel is easier after potatoes are cooked.
Yield: 1 dozen rolls

INGREDIENTS:

1 package dry yeast
¼ cup warm water
1 cup milk, scalded
½ cup sugar
1½ teaspoons salt
¼ teaspoon cinnamon
5 tablespoons butter

2 cups cooked sweet potatoes, mashed
1 teaspoon lemon juice
1 egg, slightly beaten
6 cups sifted flour
2 tablespoons butter, melted

Instructions:

Combine yeast with warm water. Stir until all dry particles are moistened. Set aside until foamy. In saucepan, scald milk. Add sugar, salt, cinnamon, and butter. Stir until butter is melted. In large bowl, combine sweet potatoes with milk mixture. Add lemon juice and beat until smooth. Cool to lukewarm. Add egg and yeast mixture and blend well. Stir in 2 cups of flour and beat at *medium* speed with electric mixer for about 3 minutes. Add enough flour to form stiff dough. On floured surface, knead until smooth. Place in buttered bowl, turning once to oil dough on all sides. Cover and allow to rise until double in bulk (1 hour). Punch down dough. Knead for 2 minutes longer and then shape into balls and place 1 inch apart on greased cookie sheet. Cover and allow dough to rise for 1 hour. Bake for 15 to 20 minutes or until golden brown. Brush tops with butter while warm.

Hot Cross Buns

Prep Time: 2 hours, 30 minutes
Cook Time: 15 minutes
Oven Temperature: 375 degrees

Preparation Tip: These rolls are yummy and rich but not sweet.
Yield: 20 buns

INGREDIENTS FOR DOUGH:

4 cups flour

1 package dry yeast

1 teaspoon cinnamon

¾ cup milk

½ cup cooking oil

⅓ cup sugar

½ teaspoon salt

3 eggs

⅔ cup raisins

½ cup walnuts

1 egg white, lightly beaten

INGREDIENTS FOR ICING:

1 tablespoon milk

¼ teaspoon almond extract

1 cup powdered sugar, sifted

Instructions:

In large mixing bowl sift together 1½ cups of flour, yeast, and cinnamon. In small saucepan heat and stir milk, oil, sugar, and salt until warm. Add to flour mixture along with eggs. Beat with electric mixer on *low* speed for 30 seconds. Increase speed to *high* for another 3 minutes. Using wooden spoon, stir in raisins and walnuts. Add as much of remaining flour as you can incorporate. On lightly floured surface, knead in enough of remaining flour to form soft dough. Place dough in greased bowl and turn once to grease dough on all sides. Cover with a towel and allow to rise until double in bulk (1½ hours). Punch dough down and return to floured surface. Cover with towel and let rise 10 minutes. Pull off pieces of dough and shape 20 smooth balls. Place 1 inch apart on greased cookie sheet. Cover and let rise until double in bulk (45 minutes). Make a crisscross slash on top of each bun. Brush with egg white and bake for 12 to 15 minutes. Cool slightly. Prepare icing by combining milk and almond extract in small bowl. Add sugar until it reaches a consistency for drizzling. Add icing along the cross marks.

Christmas Morning Pecan Rolls

Prep Time: 3 hours
Cook Time: 25 minutes
Oven Temperature: 350 degrees

Preparation Tip: These rolls are yummy and rich but not sweet.
Yield: 18 rolls

INGREDIENTS FOR DOUGH:

1 package dry yeast

2 tablespoons sugar

⅔ cup milk

3 cups flour

1 teaspoon salt

1 stick cold butter, cut into pieces

2 eggs, slightly beaten

Rind of 1 lemon, grated

INGREDIENTS FOR TOPPING:

1¼ cups dark brown sugar, firmly packed

5 tablespoons butter

½ cup water

¾ cup pecans, coarsely chopped

3 tablespoons sugar

2 teaspoons cinnamon

¾ cup raisins

INSTRUCTIONS:

Add yeast and sugar to lukewarm milk. Stir to moisten all dry particles. Set aside until foamy. Sift together flour and salt. Cut butter into flour until crumbly. Add yeast mixture, eggs, and lemon rind. Stir with wooden spoon, adding enough flour to form stiff dough. On floured surface, knead until smooth. Place in greased bowl and turn once to oil all sides of dough. Cover with towel and allow to rise until double in bulk (2 hours). In heavy saucepan, bring sugar, butter, and water to gentle boil until thick (10 minutes). Place 1 tablespoon of syrup in bottom of 18 muffin cups. Sprinkle a few pecans in each cup. Punch down dough. Return to floured surface and roll out to 18 x 12 inches. Combine sugar, cinnamon, raisins and remaining pecans. Sprinkle over dough. Roll up tightly from long side and cut into 1-inch rounds. Place in muffin cups and allow to rise another 30 minutes. Bake for 25 minutes. Invert on parchment paper. Leave 3 to 5 minutes before removing the pan.

Poppy Seed Knots

Prep Time: 4 hours
Cook Time: 25 to 30 minutes
Oven Temperature: 350 degrees

Preparation Tip: It would be a good idea to double this recipe.
Yield: 12 rolls

INGREDIENTS:

1¼ cups milk, lukewarm
4 tablespoons butter, softened
1 teaspoon sugar
1 package dry yeast
1 egg yolk

2 teaspoons salt
4 cups flour
1 egg beaten
2 teaspoons water
3 tablespoons poppy seeds

Instructions:

In a large bowl, stir together milk, butter, sugar and yeast. Set aside for 15 minutes. Stir in egg yolk, salt, and 2 cups of flour. Add an additional cup of flour and stir to form soft dough. On floured surface, knead dough, adding flour as needed, until smooth. Place in bowl, cover with towel. Let rise until double in bulk (2 hours). Punch down dough and pinch into 12 golf-ball size pieces. Roll each into rope and twist to form knot. Place 1 inch apart on greased cookie sheet. Cover and allow to rise until double in bulk (1½ hours). Combine egg and water. Brush tops of rolls. Sprinkle with poppy seeds and bake for 25 to 30 minutes.

Clover Leaf Rolls

Prep Time: 3 hours, 40 minutes
Cook Time: 20 minutes
Oven Temperature: 400 degrees

Preparation Tip: These rolls are yummy and rich but not sweet.
Yield: 24 rolls

INGREDIENTS:

1¼ cups milk, lukewarm

2 tablespoons sugar

4 tablespoons butter, softened

1 package dry yeast

1 egg

2 teaspoons salt

4 cups flour

2 tablespoons butter, melted

Instructions:

Pour lukewarm milk into large bowl and stir in sugar, butter, and yeast. Let stand for 15 minutes. Stir egg and salt into yeast mixture. Gradually stir in 3½ cups flour. Add just enough extra flour to form stiff dough. On floured surface, knead dough until smooth. Place in greased bowl, turn once to oil all sides of dough. Cover with towel and allow to rise until double in bulk (1½ hours). Punch down dough. Cut into 4 pieces. Roll each into a 14-inch rope. Cut each into 18 pieces and roll each piece into a ball. Place 3 balls of dough in each muffin cup. Cover with towel and allow to rise until double in bulk (1½ hours). Brush with butter and bake 20 minutes.

Christmas Croissants

Prep Time: 6 hours, 30 minutes
Cook Time: 10 to 12 minutes
Oven Temperature: 475 degrees

Preparation Tip: As a general rule, yeast breads should be baked toward the top of the oven.
Yield: 18 rolls

INGREDIENTS:

1 package dry yeast

1⅓ cups milk, lukewarm

2 teaspoons sugar

1½ teaspoons salt

3 to 3½ cups flour

2 sticks cold butter, cut into pieces

1 egg

2 teaspoons water

INSTRUCTIONS:

Combine yeast and warm milk in large bowl. Set aside for 15 minutes. Stir in sugar, salt, and 1 cup of flour. Gradually incorporate 2 more cups of flour, enough to form soft dough. Cover and let rise until doubled in bulk (1½ hours). On floured surface, knead dough until smooth. Wrap in waxed paper and refrigerate for 15 minutes. Roll ½ cup of butter between sheets of waxed paper to 6 x 4-inch rectangle. Repeat with second half of butter. Set aside. Roll out dough to a 12 x 8-inch rectangle. Place butter in center and fold over. Place second butter on top and fold over the top third of dough. With short side facing you, roll out to 12 x 8-inch rectangle. Wrap and refrigerate for 30 minutes. Repeat (fold, wrap, and refrigerate) three more times. Roll out to 24-inch rectangle and trim edges. Cut dough in half lengthwise and into 9 triangles to a side. Roll from base to point. Cover and let rise in refrigerator overnight. Mix egg and water. Brush tops and bake 2 minutes at 475 degrees. Lower heat to 375 degrees and bake 10 to 12 minutes.

Happy Reindeer Bread Stix

Prep Time: 2 hours
Cook Time: 20 minutes
Oven Temperature: 400 degrees

Preparation Tip: Use sesame, poppy, or caraway seeds, or no seed at all.
Yield: 20 bread sticks

INGREDIENTS:

1 package dry yeast
1¼ cups water, lukewarm
3 cups flour
2 teaspoons salt
1 teaspoon sugar

2 tablespoons olive oil
1 cup sesame seeds
1 egg, beaten
2 tablespoons sea salt

Instructions:

Combine yeast and water. Stir to moisten any dry particles. Set aside until foamy. Sift together flour, salt, and sugar. Stir in the oil. Slowly add yeast mixture and stir until it forms soft dough. Continue to add flour in small portions until it is no longer sticky. On floured surface, knead until smooth. Place in greased bowl. Turn to oil all sides of the dough. Cover and allow to rise for 45 minutes. Toast sesame seeds in skillet. Pinch off pieces of dough and roll into 12-inch ropes. Place on greased cookie sheets. Brush with egg and sprinkle with seeds and salt. Let rise, uncovered, until double in bulk (20 minutes). Bake for 15 minutes. Turn off the oven and bake for 5 minutes more.

They broke bread in their homes and
ate together with glad and sincere hearts.

ACTS 2:46 NIV

Christmas Bread Around the World

Bread, milk, and butter are of venerable antiquity.
They taste of the morning of the world.

LEIGH HUNT

CHRISTOPSOMO

Christopsomo, which translates as "Christ's bread," is a Greek bread decorated with an early form of the Christian cross with ends that split and curl into circles. Sometimes dough shapes representing initials, birth dates, ages, and aspects of the family's life and profession are added. The preparation of this special bread is considered a sacred tradition in Greek Orthodox homes and the care with which it is made is said to ensure the well-being of the home in the year to come. This rich, round loaf is traditionally baked using the most expensive ingredients and most versions are scented with wine-soaked figs, anise, and orange. It usually contains nuts, raisins, cinnamon, nutmeg, cloves, and *mastiihi*, a dried pine resin. Each region of Greece has its own variation, but most serve the bread on Christmas Eve. The head of the household blesses the loaf and each person at the table gets a slice, drizzled with honey. Families leave pieces of bread on the table believing that Christ will come and eat them during the night.

Prep Time: 4 hours
Cook Time: 45 minutes
Oven Temperature: 450 degrees for 15 minutes; 390 degrees for 25 minutes

Preparation tip: Use a mortar and pestle to crush the anise seed.
Yield: 20 to 25 servings

INGREDIENTS:

1½ tablespoons dry yeast

1 cup warm water

2 tablespoons flour

1 teaspoon salt

8 cups flour

1 cup warm red wine

½ cup olive oil

¼ cup orange juice

¼ cup water

Grated peel of 2 oranges

1 cup sugar

1½ cups raisins

1½ cups walnuts, coarsely chopped

⅓ cup pine nuts

1 tablespoon crushed anise seed

1 teaspoon ground cinnamon

1 teaspoon ground cloves

¼ teaspoon ground nutmeg

1 egg, beaten

Instructions:

Mix yeast with ½ cup warm water and 2 tablespoons flour. Stir gently until all dry particles are moistened. Let stand for 10 minutes or until surface is frothy. In large mixing bowl, sift salt with 5½ cups of flour. Make well in center of flour and pour in yeast mixture, ½ cup warm water, and wine. Mix until soft dough forms, cover with waxed paper and damp towel, and set aside to rise (about 1½ to 2 hours) until doubled in bulk. Punch the dough down and knead for several minutes until any air pockets are gone. Sift in remaining flour, add oil, orange juice, ¼ cup water, and grated orange peel. In small bowl, mix sugar, raisins, walnuts, pine nuts, anise, cinnamon, cloves, and nutmeg until blended, and add to dough. Knead well until dough is firm and doesn't stick (about 10 minutes), cover and allow to rise for an additional ½ hour. On lightly buttered baking pan, shape bread into two circular loaves, about 8 inches in diameter. Pull a fistful of dough from each loaf.

Pat dough back into shape to rise. When risen, use small pieces of dough to create designs that represent your family in some way. Place on top of the loaves. Cover with dry cloth and damp cloth over that, and place in warm place to rise again, until doubled in size. Brush with beaten egg to get a bright glaze. Place pan with 1 inch of water in the bottom of oven before preheating. Place bread in preheated oven for 15 minutes then remove pan with water, reduce heat to 390 degrees, and bake for another 25 to 30 minutes. Remove from oven, brush lightly with water, and cool on rack.

JULEKAGE

Julekage, also known as *julekaka* or *julekake*, means "Yule Bread" in Norwegian. This rich, flavorful bread is a Christmas tradition in many Scandinavian countries. Some say it originated in Norway, others say Denmark. Like many holiday breads, julekage is made with candied fruit and nuts and heavily spiced, usually with nutmeg, cinnamon, and cardamom, a spice from the ginger family, usually from India. Especially when the sweet white icing is added along with nuts, this holiday bread seems more like a Christmas cake. Most say that julekage is best right out of the oven, but it is also good toasted with butter.

Prep Time: 2 hours, 30 minutes
Cook Time: 50 minutes
Oven Temperature: 375 degrees

Preparation Tip: Brush julekage with the yolk of an egg whisked with water for a shiny, crisp surface.
Yield: 20 to 25 servings

INGREDIENTS:

2 cups mixed, diced candied fruit

1 tablespoon flour

1 stick butter

2 cups milk

½ cup water

8 cups flour, divided

2 packages rapid rise yeast

½ cup sugar

2 teaspoons salt

½ teaspoon nutmeg

½ teaspoon cinnamon

½ teaspoon ground cardamom

Milk

Instructions:

Toss candied fruit pieces in 1 tablespoon flour. Melt butter with milk and water. In large bowl, combine 4 cups of flour with yeast, sugar, salt, and spices. Add flour mixture to butter mixture and combine with electric mixer. Beat until batter falls in sheets from beaters. Fold in candied fruit. Gradually add remaining flour. Knead dough on floured surface until smooth and elastic (6 to 8 minutes). Shape dough into ball and place in greased bowl. Cover dough and let it rise in warm place (80 to 85 degrees F) until doubled in bulk (about 1 hour). Punch dough down and place on pastry board; shape into 2 loaves. Place each in greased 9 x 5 x 3-inch loaf pan. Brush tops of loaves with milk. Cover and let rise until doubled in bulk (about 45 minutes). Bake for 30 to 40 minutes or until lightly browned.

PETTOLE BREAD

Pettole are fried dough balls with their own Christmas tradition. The story goes that a woman was kneading dough when she was interrupted by sounds from outside. When she looked out, she saw shepherds hurrying by. She stopped one of the shepherds and asked where they were going. The shepherds told her that angels had appeared in the night sky and announced the birth of a baby who was even then lying in a lowly manger in Bethlehem, the city of David. The woman covered her dough and followed the shepherds. But by the time she returned, her dough was a sticky mess. The woman began to cry because she was poor and her family would have nothing to eat that day. A kind neighbor, hearing her crying, brought olive oil. When it was heated, she pinched off pieces of the dough and threw it into the oil. The result was more wonderful than they could have imagined. Even today, pettole are given to the poor at Christmastime.

Prep Time: 2 hours
Cook Time: 40 minutes

Preparation Tip: Use olive oil to fry the pettole.
Yield: 15 to 20 petolle

INGREDIENTS:

5 ¾ cups cake flour

Pinch salt

1 ounce cake of live yeast dissolved
  in warm water

1 quart warm water

Raisins, chopped dried fruit, or
  nuts (as much or as little as you
  desire)

Olive oil for frying

Powdered sugar or honey
  (optional)

Instructions:

Combine flour with salt. Add yeast and enough water to make smooth, very soft, elastic dough. It should have the consistency of thick cream. Knead dough well for about five minutes. Add raisins, chopped fruit, or nuts by stretching and restretching dough over them. Allow dough to rise in warm, draft-free place until it doubles in volume (at least an hour). The dough should be fluffier than regular bread dough.

In pot, heat enough oil (olive oil is best) for *pettole* to be completely submerged. Dip your fingers in water, pinch off and stretch out bits of dough, and drop them into hot oil. The dough will puff up and float. Flip over until both sides are golden brown. Remove them with slotted spoon and place them on absorbent paper to drain. Sprinkle with sifted powdered sugar or honey.

DATE AND ALMOND STOLLEN

Stollen or *Christstollen* is a tradition dating back to fourteenth-century Germany. The loaves were baked at Christmas to honor princes and church dignitaries, and sold at holiday fairs and festivals. Until the seventeenth century, stollen was made without milk or butter because the Catholic church did not allow these ingredients during Advent. Eventually, a papal proclamation made allowance for milk and butter, giving the bread a much improved taste. Legend has it that the shape of the stollen with the white sugar icing represents the baby Jesus wrapped in swaddling clothes, a cloth tied together by bandage-like strips. Stollen is best when eaten fresh, but it can be wrapped in foil and stored for 3 to 4 days.

Prep Time: 1 hour
Cook Time: 1 hour
Oven Temperature: 400 degrees

Preparation Tip: Stollen should be
    frosted while still warm.
Yield: 14 servings

INGREDIENTS FOR DOUGH:

¼ cup sugar

1 cup warm milk

2 packages active, dry yeast

4 cups flour

Pinch salt

2 eggs

1 stick plus 2 tablespoons butter,
    softened

½ cup almonds, coarsely chopped

Grated peel of 1 lemon

Ingredients for filling:

¼ cup cornstarch

2 cups milk

1 egg yolk

¼ cup plus 3 tablespoons sugar

1¼ cups dates, finely chopped

1 tablespoon butter

Ingredients for frosting:

1 egg white

1⅔ cups powdered sugar, sifted

Juice of 1 lemon

3 tablespoons sliced almonds, toasted

Instructions:

Stir 1 teaspoon sugar into warm milk and sprinkle with yeast. Stir gently until all dry particles are moistened. Let stand for 5 minutes or until surface is frothy. In a large bowl, sift flour and salt together. Make well in center of flour mixture and set aside. In medium bowl, whisk eggs.

Add sugar, butter, almonds, and lemon peel. Whisk together and add to flour mixture, and stir until dough forms. Knead dough on floured board until smooth (5 to 10 minutes). Cover and let rise in warm place for 30 minutes. For filling, blend cornstarch with a little milk. Then add egg yolk and sugar in medium bowl. Put dates and remaining milk into small saucepan; bring mixture to a boil. Stir milk and dates into cornstarch mixture. Add butter. Return to saucepan and bring to boil, stirring constantly until thickened. Cool, stirring occasionally to prevent a skin from forming. Knead dough on floured surface. Roll it out to a 12-inch thickness. Spread date mixture evenly over dough. Roll opposite edges to meet in center. Press them together to flatten center. Place on greased baking sheet. Let stand for 20 minutes. Bake stollen for 1 hour or until rich, brown color. For frosting, put egg white into medium bowl. Beat in powdered sugar and lemon juice. Frost and sprinkle with almonds.

THREE KINGS BREAD—TWELFTH NIGHT BREAD

By whatever name, this special bread is baked in celebration of the Day of the Three Kings, January 6. This night is set aside for exchanging Christmas presents, since tradition says it was twelve nights after the birth of the baby Jesus that the three Magi arrived bearing gifts for Him. Three Kings Bread is baked in the shape of a crown or wreath with a tiny prize inside. The prize is usually a porcelain or plastic Jesus figurine. Whoever finds the prize should expect to have good fortune throughout the year. That person is also responsible for bringing the tamales for the next party. The bread, typically decorated with candied fruit and flaked almonds, is flavored with lemon and orange zest.

Prep Time: 3 hours, 30 minutes
Cook Time: 45 minutes
Oven Temperature: 350 degrees

Preparation Tip: A silver coin or even a dry bean can be substituted for the figurine.
Yield: 14 servings

INGREDIENTS:

1 packet yeast

⅓ cup warm water

4 cups flour

1 cup sugar

4 large eggs, beaten

1½ sticks butter, warmed to room temperature

¼ teaspoon salt

1½ teaspoons cinnamon

½ teaspoon anise seed

4 teaspoons vanilla

1 small figurine

2 cups candied fruit, cut into strips

1 egg, beaten

⅓ cup sugar

Instructions:

Sprinkle yeast on surface of water and let sit for 10 minutes. Stir to moisten any dry particles remaining. In large bowl, combine yeast, flour, sugar, eggs, butter, salt, cinnamon, anise seed, and vanilla. Mix until dough forms. Knead dough for 5 minutes, then cover and let rise in warm area until dough is doubled in size (about 2 hours). Punch dough down and roll into log shape, bending ends around to form circle. Or you can make three thinner strips and braid them before pressing ends together. The wreath should be about 12 to 14 inches in diameter. Lift up one area and insert figurine by pushing it up through the bottom. Smooth out any lumps. Add dried fruit by laying it across the top and pressing it in slightly. Let it rise until doubled (about 1 hour). Brush top with egg wash, sprinkle with sugar, and bake for 45 minutes.

LUSSEKATTER

Christmas festivities in Sweden begin on December 13 with the feast of St. Lucia, the patron saint of light. Legend tells us that Lucia placed candles in a wreath on her head in order to free her arms to carry bread to Christians hiding in the catacombs. In Sweden and many other Scandinavian countries, the eldest daughter wears a white gown and a battery-operated candle wreath on her head. She leads a musical procession with her younger siblings in tow to their parent's bedroom where they present them with breakfast in bed. That breakfast consists of a special bread called *lussekatter* or St. Lucia buns. These are shaped like a figure eight and topped with raisins at either end of the spiral.

Prep Time: 2 hours
Cook Time: 15 minutes
Oven Temperature: 375 degrees

Preparation Tip: For smaller buns, divide the dough into 24 pieces.
Yield: 18 buns.

INGREDIENTS:

½ teaspoon saffron threads, finely crumbled, or 1 teaspoon powdered saffron

2 sticks butter, melted

1 cup milk

¾ cup sugar

1 teaspoon salt

2 packages dry yeast

6½ cups flour

2 eggs, well-beaten

1 egg white

½ cup golden raisins

¼ cup coarse sugar

Instructions:

Crumble saffron threads into melted butter. Set aside for up to an hour. The longer it rests, the more intense the saffron taste. Heat milk until small bubbles form across the top. Do not scald. Stir in melted butter, sugar, and salt. Pour mixture into large bowl and allow to cool until just cool enough to touch with your finger. Stir in yeast and let sit for 10 minutes. Mix half the flour into liquid. Stir in eggs. Add enough of remaining flour to form soft dough. Transfer dough to large greased bowl and turn to coat all sides. Cover with clean towel and allow to rise until doubled (about 1 hour). Punch down dough and move to floured surface. Knead lightly and pinch off small handfuls of dough. Roll into a log shape. Twist into figure eight. Place on greased cookie sheet and allow to rise until doubled (about 1 hour). Push raisins into dough at each end and brush with egg white. Bake for 15 minutes. Sprinkle with coarse sugar.

PAN DE JAMÓN

Pan de jamón is a traditional Venezuelan Christmas bread, consisting of a sweet, soft dough rolled up around savory ham, sweet raisins, and pimento-stuffed olives. It is a bread exclusive to Venezuela, created in the early 1900s as a way to use pieces of leftover holiday ham. The ham bits were marinated in wine, cinnamon, pineapples, cloves, and sugar. After baking, olives and raisins were added. In recent years, some have opted for other fillings such as bacon, salmon, or turkey. The loaf is shaped like a Swiss roll and the sugar glaze gives it a sweet, shiny finish. The bread is served as part of a traditional Christmas dinner.

Prep Time: 3 hours
Cook Time: 30 to 40 minutes
Oven Temperature: 375 degrees

Preparation Tip: For a variation, you can add 2 slices of cheddar or Swiss cheese to the filling.
Yield: 6 to 8 servings

Ingredients:

¾ cup warm milk
½ stick butter
2 tablespoons sugar
1 teaspoon salt
¼ cup lukewarm water
1 package dry yeast
3½ cups flour

1 egg, beaten
2 tablespoons butter, melted
½ pound ham, thinly sliced
½ cup raisins
½ cup pimento-stuffed olives
2 egg yolks

Instructions:

Combine milk, butter, sugar, and salt in saucepan and heat, stirring until butter melts and sugar is dissolved. Remove from heat and allow to cool to lukewarm. In small bowl, combine water and yeast. Stir to moisten any dry particles and allow to stand until foamy (5 to 10 minutes). In large bowl, combine 3 cups flour with yeast mixture, milk mixture, and beaten egg. Stir until soft dough forms. On floured surface, knead dough, adding flour as needed until dough is no longer sticky and has a silky, elastic texture. Place dough in lightly oiled bowl and turn once to bring greased side up. Cover with clean towel and set in warm place until dough doubles in size (1½ to 2 hours). Once again, place dough on floured surface and punch it down. Roll dough into rectangle about 12 inches wide and 15 inches long. Brush top of dough with melted butter. Spread ham, raisins, and olives evenly over dough, leaving a small margin on every side. Start from the bottom and roll dough into a loaf. Fold under the ends and pinch seam to seal. Place seam down on cookie sheet and cover with clean towel. Let rise for another 30 to 45 minutes. Beat egg yolks with a tablespoon of water. Brush the top with egg wash. Bake for 30 to 45 minutes.

Bunuelos

Christmas Day in Cuba was once a big celebration that included a lavish family dinner and midnight mass. Castro brought this tradition to an end when he declared Cuba an atheist country and removed Christmas from the calendar. In 1997, in honor of a visit by Pope John Paul II, Castro reestablished Christmas as a national holiday. However, in Cuba, Christmas is still like any other day. Businesses are open and children attend school. In the U.S. Cuban-Americans celebrate as in the old days. Full-scale preparations begin on Christmas Eve, a workday committed to cooking, baking, and setting up for the big party. The holiday feast typically consists of roast pig, black beans, and rice. Parties last late into the night with party-goers moving from house to house. *Bunuelos*—one of the most popular Cuban holiday breads—is a type of sweet fried dough topped with powdered sugar or a sweet syrup. Though many Latin countries feature a form of bunuelos, the Cuban version is by far the most elaborate. Traditional bunuelos contain a number of tropical vegetables such as yucca, alum, and white sweet potatoes not easily obtained in standard markets. A simpler version of this tasty bread has been included.

Prep Time: 30 minutes
Cook Time: 3 to 5 minutes on each side
Total Time: 40 minutes

Preparation Tip: Bunuelos can be sprinkled with powdered sugar, coarse cane sugar, or syrup.
Yield: 12 to 14 servings

INGREDIENTS FOR BUEUELOS:

2⅓ cups flour

⅓ teaspoon baking powder

¼ cup cinnamon sugar, powdered sugar, or coarse cane sugar

⅔ teaspoon salt

½ stick butter

1⅓ whole eggs

⅓ cup milk

Canola oil for frying

INGREDIENTS FOR SYRUP:

½ stick butter

1 cup sugar

¼ cup water

2 tablespoons rum extract

INSTRUCTIONS:

Sift together flour, baking powder, sugar, and salt. Cut butter into flour mixture. In separate bowl, beat eggs and milk together until smooth. Add milk mixture to flour mixture. Work until soft dough forms. On floured surface, knead dough until smooth. Break off small pieces and roll into balls. Fry in canola oil, turning until all sides are brown. Drain on paper towel. To prepare syrup, melt butter in saucepan. Add sugar, water, and rum extract. Bring to slow boil. Reduce heat to medium and cook for 10 minutes. Let cool. Pour over bunuelos and let them stand for 1 hour to absorb syrup.

ENGLISH CHRISTMAS BREAD

In years gone by, English families around the country typically sat down to Christmas dinner at the same time so they would be finished and ready to watch the Queen's speech broadcast on the "telly" at 3:00 p.m. These days, the Queen records her speech, and it is played a number of times during the course of the day. This allows Christmas dinnertimes to be less rigid. Other than the time, however, the traditional Christmas meal is pretty much the same, beginning with smoked salmon and bacon-wrapped prawns. Roast turkey or goose makes up the main course. The Brits also indulge in a delicious Christmas Bread eaten throughout the day.

Prep Time: 4 hours
Cook Time: 1 hour
Oven Temperature: 325 degrees

Preparation Tip: Rising times will vary.
Yield: 12 to 14 servings

INGREDIENTS:

¼ cup citron, chopped

¼ cup raisins, chopped

1 package yeast

¼ cup warm water

3 cups flour

¼ cup sugar

1 teaspoon salt

¼ teaspoon nutmeg

½ teaspoon allspice

½ teaspoon caraway seed

½ stick butter

Instructions:

Combine raisins and citron together; set aside. Soften yeast in warm water. Sift together 1 cup of flour, sugar, salt, spices, and caraway seed. Cut in butter with pastry blender. Form well in flour mixture and add yeast mixture. Add milk and stir until smooth. Blend in half the remaining flour and fruit. Add the rest of the flour gradually to make soft dough. Turn dough out on lightly floured surface and knead until smooth. Place dough in greased bowl and turn once to bring greased side up. Cover and let rise in warm place until double in size (1½ to 2 hours). Turn dough out on floured surface, knead, and shape into 2 loaves. Place in greased pans 6 x 3.5 x 2.25–inches. Let rise until double in size (½ hour). Bake for 1 hour.

CHRISTMAS HOUSKA

In the Czech Republic, Christmas lasts for three days, with most of the festivities taking place on Christmas Eve. In preparation, houses are thoroughly cleaned, carpets washed, and furniture dusted. On the big day, families spend all day together decorating the Christmas tree and preparing a wonderful Christmas dinner that typically consists of carp and potato salad or fish soup. Dinner, which is followed by shopping and midnight mass, is served as soon as the first star appears in the evening sky. The bread of the day is called *Houska* or *Vanochka*. It is a braided, egg-based fruit bread that resembles the Jewish Challah bread. It is best when served warm with butter, jelly, or confectioner's sugar.

Prep Time: 2 hour, 45 minutes
Cook Time: 40 to 45 minutes
Oven Temperature: 325 degrees

Preparation Tip: Use toothpicks to hold this braided bread in place while baking.
Yield: 8 to 10 servings

INGREDIENTS:

1 cup milk
½ cup shortening
¾ cup sugar
¾ teaspoon salt
2 packages dry yeast
¼ cup warm water
2 eggs, beaten
5½ cups flour, sifted

¼ cup raisins
¼ cup citron, chopped
¼ cup almonds, blanched and
   chopped
2 tablespoons butter, melted
1 egg
1 tablespoon water
¼ cup almonds, blanched

INSTRUCTIONS:

In small saucepan, scald milk. Stir in shortening, sugar, and salt. Cool to lukewarm.

In large bowl, sprinkle yeast into ¼ cup water. Stir until all the dry particles are moistened and let stand until foamy. Stir in milk mixture, eggs, and 3 cups of flour until smooth. Add raisins, citron, chopped almonds, and enough flour to make a stiff dough (about 2½ cups). Place dough on floured surface and knead until smooth. Place in greased bowl, turning to grease all sides. Cover with towel and let rise in warm place until double in bulk (about 1 to 1½ hours). Punch down dough.

Return to the floured surface and divide into 6 pieces. Using your hands, roll each piece into 18-inch strips. Place strips 1 inch apart on greased cookie sheet. Begin in the middle and braid to each end. Let rise in warm place about 1 hour or until double in bulk. Beat together egg and water and brush the top of the dough. Decorate with whole almonds. Bake for 40 to 45 minutes. Best when served slightly warm.

POTICA

In Slovenia, the Christmas holiday is typically marked by the burning of incense, sprinkling of holy water, and special foods, like the Christmas loaf called *potica*. This Christmas bread resembles a nut roll, consisting of a sweet yeast dough rolled out thin and spread with a nut paste made from ground nuts and a sweetener, usually honey. The dough is then rolled into a log shape, sometimes left long and straight and other times bent into a horseshoe shape. It is baked and sliced crosswise. Though it may look like a nut roll, *potica* has more layers of dough and filling, but fewer layers than strudels. *Orehova*, which means walnuts, are the most common type of nut used.

Prep Time: 2 hours, 30 minutes
Cook Time: 40 to 45 minutes
Oven Temperature: 350 degrees

Preparation Tip: Walnuts should be
ground in a food processor rather than
chopped by hand.
Yield: 24 to 28 servings

INGREDIENTS FOR DOUGH:

2 packages dry yeast

½ cup warm water

2 cups scalded milk

¾ cup sugar

1 tablespoon salt

1 stick butter

4 egg yolks

1 to 9 cups flour

Ingredients for Filling:

1 cup light cream

1 pound of shelled walnuts, finely
  ground

1½ cups sugar

1 teaspoon salt

1 teaspoon vanilla

½ stick butter

¼ cup fresh bread crumbs

4 egg whites

Instructions:

In a small bowl, sprinkle yeast into warm water and stir until all dry particles are moistened. Let set until foamy. In a saucepan, heat milk until scalded. Add sugar, salt, and butter. Stir until smooth. Allow to cool to lukewarm. Stir in the egg whites, yeast mixture, and 2 cups of flour. Mix well. Stir enough flour to make stiff dough. On lightly floured surface, knead dough until smooth. Place in greased bowl, turning once to grease all sides. Cover with a clean towel; let rise in a warm place until double in bulk (about 1 hour). Make filling by heating cream to boil in medium saucepan. Remove from heat and stir in ground walnuts, sugar, salt, and vanilla. In another saucepan, melt butter and stir in bread crumbs until lightly browned. Add to walnut mixture. Beat egg whites until stiff and fold in walnut mixture. Turn dough onto floured surface and divide into 4 parts. *Do not knead*. Roll each piece into 16 x 9-inch rectangle. Spread with walnut filling. Roll up like a jelly roll, starting from short side. Pinch ends and side to seal. Place each in greased 4.9 x 5 x 3-inch loaf pan. Let rise for 1 hour. Bake for 40 to 45 minutes.

IRISH SODA BREAD

The Irish love their bread. Soda bread, a crusty brown bread made from whole-wheat flour and buttermilk is a national treasure. During the Christmas season, raisins and caraway seeds are added to make it a festive part of Irish holiday tradition. After dinner on Christmas Eve, the table is set once again. A plate with the holiday soda bread is placed in the center, along with a pitcher of milk. A glowing candle decorates the window, and the door is left unlocked. This ritual is a gesture of hospitality to the Holy Family, that they might find rest and comfort from those who dwelt within. This hospitality extends to travelers who might need food or shelter from the elements.

Prep Time: 30 minutes
Cook Time: 35 minutes
Oven Temperature: 425 degrees for 5 minutes, 250 degrees for 30 minutes

Preparation Tip: Remove foil from top of loaf for last 10 minutes of baking to allow for browning.
Yield: 10 to 12 servings

INGREDIENTS:

5 cups flour

1 cup sugar

1 tablespoon baking powder

1½ teaspoons salt

1 teaspoon baking soda

1 stick unsalted butter, cut into cubes, room temperature

2½ cups raisins

3 tablespoons caraway seeds

2½ cups buttermilk

1 large egg

Instructions:

In large bowl, whisk together flour, sugar, baking powder, salt, and baking soda. Add butter. Using fingertips, rub in until coarse crumbs form. Stir in raisins and caraway seeds. Whisk together buttermilk and egg in medium bowl. Add to dough. Stir until sticky dough is formed. Transfer dough to floured surface and lightly knead. Form into round loaf. Place loaf on greased cookie sheet. Dip small knife in flour and cut 1-inch-deep X on the top center of dough. Lay piece of foil over loaf.

Bake at 425 degrees for 5 minutes. Lower heat and bake at 250 degrees for 30 minutes. Remove foil and bake for another 10 minutes. Place on wire rack to cool. Wrap in foil and store at room temperature. Serve with lots of butter.

OPLATEK

The traditional Christmas dinner in Poland—a 12-course meal called *Wigilia*—is served on Christmas Eve. A white tablecloth is spread over a thin layer of hay, and an extra place is set at the table in case a stranger knocks on the door. It is also a reminder of absent loved ones. The meal begins with the breaking of the *oplatek*, a thin, wafery bread intended to symbolize the family's daily bread and common life. The head of the family offers a prayer and gives pieces of the oplatek to each person, wishing them joy in the upcoming year because the Christ Child has been born. The meal is often followed by a reading of the nativity story from the Bible. The oplatek bread is treasured not so much for its taste as for the spiritual truths it symbolizes.

Prep Time: 30 minutes
Cook Time: 20 to 30 minutes
Oven Temperature: 375 degrees

Preparation Tip: Refrigerating flour and water prior to combining may produce best results.
Yield: About 20 wafers

INGREDIENTS:

1 cup flour

1 cup powdered sugar

¼ teaspoon saffron

2 egg whites

3 to 4 tablespoons water

Instructions:

Sift together flour, sugar, and saffron. Add egg whites and water. On floured surface, knead for 5 to 8 minutes until stiff dough is formed. Let dough rest for 10 minutes and then knead it again. Roll dough as thinly as possible and cut into squares or circles. Place on greased cookie sheet. Bake for 20 to 30 minutes or until cooked through. Cook time will vary with the thickness of the dough. Wrap in plastic wrap and store in an air-tight container until ready to serve.

Notes

Notes

Notes

Notes

Notes

Notes

Notes

Notes

Notes

Notes

Notes

Notes

Notes

Index

Thanks be to God for
His indescribable gift!

2 CORINTHIANS 9:15 NKJV